THE MID-SUFFOLK
LIGHT RAILWAY

BY

N. A. COMFORT

THE OAKWOOD PRESS

THE MID-SUFFOLK LIGHT RAILWAY

THE heart of East Suffolk has changed little in the last few centuries; the scenery is magnificent: rolling hills and cornfields, while the villages contain much fine architecture, such as the "wool" church at Laxfield; from this area came such men as Grosseteste, Bishop of Lincoln, and Sancroft, Archbishop of Canterbury. This same area has always been thinly populated, and nothing larger than what we now would call a village has ever appeared; there are few enough of these: Laxfield, Mendlesham and Debenham are probably the largest and all are comparatively remote.

This lack of centres of population caused a large gap to be left in the railway map. All round the area lines were built: Ipswich-Bury (1846), Haughley-Norwich (1848-9), Halesworth-Haddiscoe (1854), Tivetshall-Harleston (1855), Ipswich-Halesworth, Haddiscoe-Yarmouth, Framlingham and Snape branches, Saxmundham-Leiston and Beccles-Lowestoft (these last were all opened on June 1st, 1859). These were followed by Leiston-Aldeburgh (1860), Harleston-Beccles (1860-3), Mellis-Eye (1867), Haddiscoe spur (1872) and Forncett-Wymondham (1881). A line through central East Suffolk was now conspicuous by its absence, but the Great Eastern, with its precarious finances, was not in a position to finance any dubious railway scheme when its own road cartage service in the area seemed adequate. In spite of this, a short branch leading southwards from Pulham Market was constructed by the G.E.R.; although it only led to a farm, it could have been extended southwards into the centre of the county had any objective warranted it.

Light railways were planned in large numbers after the 1896 Act, many concerned having been only waiting for the Bill to become law. Not all of the plans materialised, but the Mid-Suffolk scheme was one that did. An abortive attempt to start a company had been made in 1889, but the Mid-Suffolk Light Railway Company was not incorporated until October 1900. It was empowered to raise capital of £300,000 in debenture and preference shares, as was then the custom. (This proved the principal cause of the downfall of the company). The plans put forward were approved by a Light Railway Order of 1901 and the total length of the line, sanctioned under the terms of the Act, was to be forty-two miles.

The Company, according to their prospectus, also proposed the running of buses by the Company from Westerfield station to the town centre of Ipswich, presumably in competition with Great Eastern trains and perhaps with Ipswich Corporation trams as well. This service would have been convenient, as Ipswich station is some way from the town centre. There seems to have been considerable local opposition to the original plans, especially in the Mendlesham area, and the Company altered their original plans in many cases.

The Chairman of the Company was Mr. F. S. Stevenson, M.P., and with him on the board were the Earl of Stradbroke, J.B. Chevallier, J. D. Cobbold and F. M. Remnant. The line was seen by the *East Anglian Daily Times* as starting from Westerfield station on the G.E.R. line from Ipswich to Saxmundham, and running to Halesworth (G.E.R. and Southwold Railway), with a branch from Kenton to Haughley, on the Ipswich-Ely line. It would thus fill in the large triangle of undeveloped farming land between these two arms of the Great Eastern stretching out into Suffolk northwest and north-east from Ipswich. The company's own advertisement for the ceremony of cutting the first sod, however, saw the railway as running from Haughley to Halesworth with a branch to Westerfield, and this doubt about the precise purposes of the undertaking continued.

Be that as it may, the ceremony itself was performed in a field just north of Westerfield G.E.R. station, and what a show it was. Present were H.R.H. the Duke of Cambridge, the Marquis and Marchioness of Bristol (the gentleman after whom most of the Hotels Bristols of Europe are named), Lord Claud Hamilton, Chairman of the Great Eastern, Lords Rayleigh and Huntingfield, Sir Charles Dalrymple, and a host of other great names, with the bands of the First Suffolks and the Volunteer Artillery. The date was 3 May 1902. His Royal Highness made a speech, the theme of which was that the country should not go too fast; changes should be made gradually: "We are too fond these days of rushing". He could not have been more prophetic. However, the sod cut by the ceremonial spade was deposited in the highly ornate wheelbarrow, and the six hundred lucky holders of red and gilt lunch tickets sat down to a large meal in a big marquee equipped with six carving tables.

On 5 May 1902 the *East Anglian Daily Times* reported: "Into the night of Mid-Suffolk, Mr. F. S. Stevenson has flung the stone—has been the principal means of starting a light railway". This allusion to a well-known line in "Omar Khayyam", which had been translated by the Suffolk poet Fitzgerald, was prophetic in that it brought into focus the essentially county character of the line and the dreamlike quality of its objectives. It was inspired by the ceremony of cutting the first sod; what the writer did not know was that the point at which the ceremony took place would never see track, let alone trains, that it would be six long years before even a portion of the railway was fully open, and that two of the directors standing there would be virtually beggared by the undertaking. Never again, alas, would the great of the land single out this little line for their special attention.

The contractors appointed (on 11 January 1902) were Messrs. Jackson & Co., and they were instructed to begin simultaneously at Haughley and at Westerfield; the cost was to be £5,300 per mile. Work did in fact start at the former place but not at the latter. Indeed, work at Haughley may have started before the ceremony mentioned above, for as early as 23 September 1902, General Viscount Kitchener paid a ceremonial visit to the Mid-Suffolk Light Railway and was carried from Mendlesham to Haughley in a train comprising contractors' wagons and a G.E.R. saloon, hauled by the Manning Wardle saddle-tank *Lady Stevenson*, named after the mother of the Chairman. Could this track have been laid in four months? Doubtful, surely? Lord Kitchener had spent the night at Aspall after a reception at Ipswich, and went on by road to join the train at Mendlesham; on arrival at Haughley, he drank a glass of champagne and went off with a cortege of horseless carriages to Stowmarket.

In February 1903 the local press reported that much satisfaction had been expressed in the neighbourhood of Worlingworth, Stradbroke

A NEW LIGHT RAILWAY IN EAST ANGLIA: THE DUKE OF CAMBRIDGE CUTTING THE FIRST SOD OF THE MID-SUFFOLK LINE.

A contemporary sketch of the ceremony at Westerfield.

and Laxfield at the pegging out of the actual route from Kenton to Halesworth. All was, unfortunately, not well. Difficulties arose over the section from Huntingfield to Halesworth, particularly in regard to the approach over the marshy ground to the south-west of the town, and an order was applied for to cover a deviation. The hearing was held at the Angel Hotel at Halesworth on 14 July 1903, under Col. Boughey and H. A. Steward. The new line was to be one mile shorter than the former one, and would skirt Halesworth on the north-west and terminate to the north of the G.E. station, but to the west of the railway, with another deviation of one furlong making a junction with the G.E.R. main line. The Great Eastern objected to the scheme because goods trains would have to be exchanged on a gradient of 1 in 70 (1 in 96 according to the M.S.L.R. counsel) and trains off the light railway would have to cross both G.E.R. running lines to reach the main sidings. The application was granted, but it may be mentioned here that in 1907 when the Company came back to the Light Railway Commissioners, they confessed that they were badly advised about the deviation, that it would cost a great deal more than they expected or could afford, and asked for a third alternative to be accepted, namely of crossing over the G.E.R. south of Halesworth and running by the Southwold Railway (a narrow gauge line) for half a mile into a station to the east of the other two. The M.S.L.R. had unfortunately already constructed earthworks at Halesworth in accordance with the original scheme.

Meanwhile, work was progressing, but slowly. In 1903 the directors resolved that "the contractors shall proceed with their work from Kenton Junction simultaneously towards Halesworth and towards Westerfield, but more rapidly towards the former than towards the latter", and that all fences should be erected as soon as possible with the exception of those on the Halesworth deviation.

Liaison between the board and Jacksons was getting steadily worse. No wonder that when the chairman of Kenton parish meeting wrote to the company proposing extensions to Eye, Framlingham and Saxmundham, the company had to reply that it had no intention of doing so! The quarrels were over many things: fences were not erected, light and heavy work were done together instead of separately as planned, and the contractors had even forgotten to provide a water supply for the locomotives. The situation deteriorated rapidly: the Board wanted the Laxfield and Debenham sections open by the end of September 1904; but nearly all the capital had been spent with only half the line finished, and legal action was considered against the contractors. By 13 July 1903, however, it was possible to run a special train comprising a G.E.R. saloon and wagons from Haughley to Mendlesham, where it picked up Mr. Stevenson and the band of the Forresters, and on to Horham; here, because the track ahead was only just laid, the party changed to a contractors' train and went on to Laxfield.

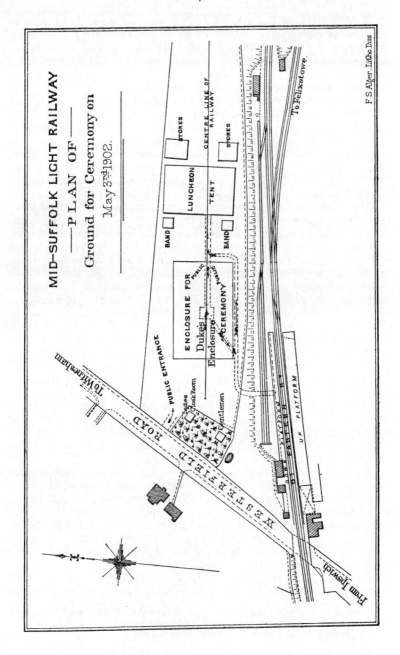

In May 1904 the Company was very short of money, and went to East Suffolk County Council for a loan of £25,000 which would suffice to complete the lines to Westerfield and Halesworth. The proposal was defeated by twenty-seven votes to twenty-four (it would have needed a two-thirds majority). Nevertheless, at the July Annual Meeting, the Chairman was encouraging, saying that the lines to Laxfield and Debenham would be ready by September and to Halesworth by February 1905. He referred to the arrangements he had made with the G.E.R. for covered ways to join the stations at Westerfield and Halesworth and to the use of steam rail motors, drawing from experience with these on the Taff Vale Railway the conclusion that operating costs would be 5½d. per mile. The contractors were at that time working on the bridge over the Aspall road at Debenham, and fencing was being done as far as Linstead on the main line and Otley on the branch.

The line was finally opened for goods traffic on 20 September 1904 from Haughley to Mendlesham, Aspall, Kenton, Horham, Stradbroke and Laxfield. It is known that rails had also been laid from Kenton down the branch to within 150 yards of Debenham station, and it seems that goods traffic to this point must have been allowed, for in 1906 there was a complaint that the facility for the public to "load and unload" at Debenham had been withdrawn. It is usually stated that no part of the Westerfield branch was ever opened, and whether this brief and no doubt semi-official traffic from Kenton to Debenham constituted an opening must be left to historical quidnuncs. For a period the contractor's offices were located at Debenham, on the branch. Mr. Frederick Moore, who worked on the construction of the line, recalled some years ago in an article in the *East Anglian* that he used to lodge in a cottage on the Aspall Road at Debenham, and was picked up every morning by the train comprising *Lady Stevenson**, some wagons, and a pay office made from an open wagon. The first track was flat-bottomed on half-round sleepers, with sand ballast; some track was laid straight on the top-soil and simply ballasted over. The earthworks were constructed with the help of two-foot gauge track worked by horses with tip trucks.

At this time the intention of the company was to employ a loco-motive for freight traffic and market specials, and a steam railcar for normal passenger traffic, and to order ten goods wagons. While the latter were constructing, trucks were hired from the Great Eastern. There was one daily freight train and as the advertisement stated that "the traffic will be worked by the Railway Company", it seems that the locomotive *Haughley* (believed to have been the first of the three Hudswell Clarke 0-6-0T engines) had already arrived.

The Board carried out a survey of freight traffic available; with extreme optimism, the Company believed the long-term prospects to

---

* *Lady Stevenson* was precisely similar to Messrs. Pauling and Sons' *Penn* (built 1902), and was in the same livery with cast name plate and cast number plate "No. 7" below; it may have been hired from Paulings.

OPENING OF THE LINE FOR GOODS TRAFFIC.

For the convenience of the Public, and as a temporary arrangement, it has been decided to OPEN PART OF THIS LINE for *Goods, Live Stock, and Parcels Traffic,*

On TUESDAY, September 20th, 1904,

When the following Stations will be available, viz :—

HAUGHLEY	**HORHAM**
MENDLESHAM	**STRADBROKE**
ASPALL	**LAXFIELD**
KENTON	

Your attention is particularly directed to the fact that at present the *Stations will only be open at specified times,* as per accompanying Time Table, and that Traffic can only be dealt with at those times.

Trucks will be left at the various Stations, and can be unloaded at once.

Advise Notes of Traffic awaiting delivery will be sent to Consignees.

A List of Parcels awaiting delivery will be displayed at each Station.

Particulars can be obtained from the Officials at the time the Trains are at the various Stations, or from

Mr. H. L. GODDEN, General Manager, FRAMSDEN Stowmarket.

Mr. H. J. REDNALL, Traffic Manager, HAUGHLEY, Stowmarket.

Mr. H. R. GILLINGWATER, Assistant Manager, HAUGHLEY, Stowmarket.

Mr. T. H. BRYANT, Local Secretary, LAXFIELD, Framlingham.

TIME TABLE.

		A.M.				P.M.
HAUGHLEY,	.... depart	**8.0**	**LAXFIELD,**	.... depart		**1.0**
Mendlesham,	.... arrive	**8.20**	**Stradbroke,**	.... arrive		**1.15**
	.... depart	**8.40**		.... depart		**1.35**
Aspall, ...	.... arrive	**9.5**	**Horham,**	.... arrive		**1.42**
	.... depart	**9.25**		.... depart		**2.2**
Kenton, ...	.... arrive	**9.30**	**Kenton,**	.... arrive		**2.32**
	.... depart	**9.45**		.... depart		**2.47**
Horham, ...	.... arrive	**10.15**	**Aspall,**	.... arrive		**2.52**
	.... depart	**10.35**		.... depart		**3.12**
Stradbroke,	.... arrive	**10.42**	**Mendlesham,**	.... arrive		**3.36**
	.... depart	**11.0**		.... depart		**3.55**
LAXFIELD,	.... arrive	**11.15**	**HAUGHLEY,**	.... arrive		**4.15**

be good; the Board was quite prepared to wait until the entire system was completed before they inaugurated the passenger service, and freight and parcels, which were dealt with from the start, were in fact self-supporting in that receipts covered bare running costs. It appears that Wilby station was not opened at this time, and Gipping station, or Old Newton as it was then known, was intended to have handled passengers at a later date.

The first staff dinner was held at the Queen's Head at Stradbroke in mid-February, after a press tour of the line by goods train, and optimism was again the key-note. In January the Company had carried 1,500 tons of goods, 30 trucks of cattle, and 500 parcels. At this time an early cattle-train for the Ipswich market was started, leaving Haughley at 4.30 a.m., but in fact the area was turning from cattle to corn, and this traffic did not develop as hoped.

At the 1905 Annual Meeting, it was announced that the Company now owned two engines, seven carriages (apparently ex-Metropolitan District coaches modified for operation as vestibule carriages, but without covered connections); two brake vans, two horse-boxes, six cattle wagons and 18 open trucks. Reference was made to disputes with the contractors, which were likely to go to arbitration. Meanwhile the Company had gone cap in hand to the Halesworth Council, from whom they had extracted a promise of a loan of £5,000, to be backed by a further £5,000 from the Treasury. But the debenture holders blocked this move; indeed the edifice was already toppling. Mr Stevenson retired from the chairmanship and in May 1906 was declared bankrupt.

From the public examination of this unfortunate ex-chairman, it appeared that some £95,000 of his money had been lost in the line. The ordinary shares were now selling at 57s. 6d. per £10, and debentures were withdrawn at an auction at this time after the biggest offer was £57. Moreover, he had apparently agreed to purchase £100,000 of Great Eastern stock (he made a loss of £30,000 on the deal) with the object of bringing about friendly relations with that line, and so getting through rates; as the G.E.R. had suspected that Mr. Stevenson was acting on behalf of the Midland Railway to open the way for this acquisitive line to Suffolk, this heavy investment would have presumably proved on whose side his allegiance lay. Mr. Stevenson certainly had been acquiring control of Midland Railway shares as well, but would not commit himself as to the purpose of the deals. The debtor made no bones that he had been living on his wife's income since 1889, and on money left him by his step-father, and described himself as never having been in business, but having spent the greater part of his life in study, and in publishing certain works, the copyright of which was of no value. He also agreed that in the final stages he was buying jewellery on credit and pawning it the same day; this process, and payments to money lenders, lost him a further £45,000.

This was the man who had been regarded as the father of the Mid-Suffolk! The Official Receiver said: "You put all your eggs in one basket and other people's as well". And indeed he had even realised his mother's trust fund. Sympathy for a man in such straits may be excused; but how could the fortunes of a railway be given over to someone of such blundering inadequacy in business? The answer must be that local connections were all; this M.P. for Eye with the big house at Woodbridge was easily acceptable. Stevenson continually declared that he had accepted control of the Mid-Suffolk with reluctance, and he may in fact have regarded the job as an obligation. Although he had purchased land at Kenton, nothing came out to suggest that he had put his own future before that of the railway. It must be remembered, too, that M.Ps were still unpaid when the bankruptcy occurred.

At the 1906 General Meeting the forecasts were more subdued than previously; the new Chairman, the Earl of Stradbroke, replied to a questioner regarding the opening from Debenham to Westerfield that "they had better try to get to Halesworth first". The contractor had been changed, and reading between the lines it looks as if work had virtually stopped. Freight services were extended to Cratfield, the metals having been in place for over a year, but in May the next year a Receiver and Manager was called in. All construction was now halted, although little had been done in the previous two and a half years.

The main reasons for the Company's troubles had appeared at the February 1907 Hearing of the second deviation application previously referred to. The failure of the chairman, which resulted in there being £20,000 of promissory notes which were worthless, had come at the same time as an abortive inspection by the Board of Trade to consider whether the line was fit for passenger traffic. The answer was that it was not, and to make it fit would cost £5,000. This was due to failure by the contractor to do his job properly, but on applying to them to put it right, he found himself unable to do so. Arbitration followed, and the contractors were disposed of, with some saving of money to the railway.

But, as counsel pointed out, they had a railway "from an ascertained point to a dead-end" on which they could only work freight traffic. This traffic was showing a profit of £500 per annum, but the debenture interest was in arrears. Application had been made for loans from local authorities, but the Light Railway Commissioners would only allow this if the debenture holders permitted these to rank *pari-passu* with debentures already issued. This the holders refused to do and after allowing interest to be held over another six months, the largest debenture holder applied to the courts for a Receiver to be appointed.

Incidentally, the alarm shown by counsel for the Great Eastern at this hearing is not difficult to explain. Plans had been drawn up showing a triangular junction of the second deviation route with the Southwold undertaking's line south of Halesworth, although counsel for the

M.S.L.R. was at pains to say that his clients had no intention of running along Southwold tracks, except with that company's approval (and the Southwold were objectors). At this time talk was going on about the development of the river at Walberswick, which resulted a few years later in the opening of the Blackshore Quay on the Southwold side of the river and a Southwold Railway branch thereto. The Great Eastern counsel painted a picture of this "port" open, with a facing junction to the M.S.L.R. at Halesworth off a Southwold railway converted to standard gauge and of fish traffic pouring by this route on to the Mid-Suffolk. The fact that the ex-chairman of the Mid-Suffolk had been dealing in Midland Railway shares was known and the spectre of Southwold becoming another Harwich within the Midland empire was not by any means unimaginable.

Somehow, it seems, enough money was found to put the track in good enough trim to pass the Board of Trade Inspector and a passenger service was introduced between Haughley and Laxfield only, using the second-hand carriages in mixed trains, calling at Gipping (freight only), Mendlesham, Brockford & Wetheringsett, Aspall & Thorndon, Kenton Junction, Worlingworth, Horham, Stradbroke and Wilby. The first train to carry passengers officially was the 7.35 a.m. mixed train ex-Haughley for Laxfield on 29 September 1908, just four years after the line had been opened with such high hopes.

In May 1909 the *Halesworth Advertiser* reported that great satisfaction was being expressed in the district that the Mid-Suffolk Light Railway was depositing the plans with the Light Railway Commissioners for an extension of the line to Halesworth. This, unless a fourth alternative has come to light (none has been published) must have been a further attempt to get approval for the 1907 deviation plans, but it is the last that was heard of any intention to extend.

Not long afterwards, contraction set in. In February 1912 the freight-only Cratfield section was abandoned and trains ran only half a mile past Laxfield, to Laxfield Mills, where goods continued to be handled. Although this branch was officially only for freight traffic, engines ran down to the water tower, sometimes light but often with coaches. No passengers are recorded as having been carried, but the Suffolk people's friendly and carefree nature makes it likely that passengers were carried on unofficial trains throughout the system. During the First World War some three and a half miles of abandoned track were lifted, from Laxfield Mills to Cratfield and from Kenton towards Debenham. No further track-work, other than replacements, were laid, apart from the construction of new sidings at Haughley during the Second World War. By now, the company's future was grim: by 1921 £205,894 out of the maximum possible £300,000 had been spent on half the system, the estimated cost of the whole of which had been around £225,000.

The takeover by the London and North Eastern Railway at the grouping imposed by the Railways Act of 1921, probably saved the line from a much quicker end. The only difference from independent operating was the increase in through running; on occasion trains ran through to Stowmarket and L.N.E.R. goods vans began to work through to the branch. The original rolling stock was replaced by some that was a little less prehistoric. Passenger traffic, never heavy, had begun to decline during the 1920's. Goods traffic, cattle, grain, roadstone, fruit, dairy produce and coal declined as the line was challenged by road transport and the services slowly pruned in consequence. It was much quicker to go anywhere by car, as the trains were delayed by shunting at most stations. Even at the height of the line's prosperity, traffic rarely exceeded 1,000 tons per week of freight or 600 head of cattle.

Traffic picked up again in the Second World War, as basic petrol was withdrawn and bus companies cut rural services drastically and pooled vehicles. As soon as the war was over and traffic to Mendlesham was beginning to fall off, things became worse than ever. By the time nationalisation took the line into the British Railways' system, there was only one engine in steam for a good deal of the time. Traffic continued to fall and it was evident that the line could not last long.

Eventually the line was scheduled for closure on Monday, 28 July 1952. It actually closed on the 26th, as the 27th was a Sunday and no Sunday trains had run since 1921. The last week was the busiest for years, many people who had not travelled on the line for years coming to pay their last respects to the "Middy". Trains were packed and on the last day an engine broke down on the main line while hauling a connection for the last train, making it leave Haughley at 4.48 p.m. instead of 3.55 p.m. as scheduled. The Haughley stationmaster had made special arrangements to cope with the crowds and a temporary refreshment room was opened.

The train plodded towards Laxfield, both two-car sets filled, and in spite of photostops and other unscheduled halts, time was recovered. When the train reached Laxfield, it would normally have spent the weekend there, but as there were around three hundred revellers wanting to return and only a few wagons to be cleared, an extra train was put on. Among the passengers was a party of people dressed in clothes that might have been worn at the opening in 1908: 65447 managed well on the way back to gain more time. The return journey followed the formula generally followed nowadays: detonators were exploded at most stations, while at Mendlesham a loudspeaker van played "Auld Lang Syne". The engine ran to Ipswich with the rolling stock and the Mid-Suffolk Light Railway had carried its last official train.

Little now remains of the line. Some time later the track was lifted and the land sold. Silos now stand near Aspall, where rose-framed nameboards once told the traveller that he was miles from anywhere, but at Laxfield the M.S.L.R. buildings can still be seen in much of their shabby glory.

A DESCRIPTION OF THE LINE

The outstanding feature of the Mid-Suffolk was the large number of road and occupation crossing places; there were 114 between Haughley and Laxfield Station alone and many more planned on the remainder, although not as many in proportion as the ground was less level. Most crossings were merely occupation crossings and the L.N.E.R. dismissed most of the seven crossing keepers who had worked the line in 1924, when 86 crossings had been "occupation", 11 managed by station staff and 12 ungated. At the end, residents frequently lent a hand and crews were often officially responsible for opening and closing gates for themselves.

Until the groupings and for some time afterwards, the M.S.L.R. had its own station at Haughley and freight traffic was funnelled through exchange sidings between the two stations to the main line. The old station, a single platform with a station office, stood above the main station to the east and was demolished during the Second World War, when the branch trains began to run from the up side bay platform of the main station; new exchange sidings were built on the station site. This enabled the passengers to connect without having to do more than cross the platform.

The "Middy" ran northwards from Haughley station for a very short distance before turning sharply east, leaving the main line which divides a little further northwards. The line ran up a 1 in 42 bank, over one of the rare underbridges (over Haugh Lane) for $1\frac{1}{2}$ miles to Gipping siding, once known as Old Newton, which was so far from a village that even the M.S.L.R. Board did not think it a paying proposition for passengers. Here a little agricultural produce was occasionally dealt with.

After rising a little further, the line fell towards Mendlesham. Here was an instance of the contractors' habit of overruling the Board on the question of what should be done. At Mendlesham Ford the Board had wished a bridge to be built over the road, but as the contractors would do nothing, a level crossing was substituted. Mendlesham station, although serving a largish village, did not contribute much to traffic, as it was near the main Ipswich-Norwich road. Most trains were timed to do these first $4\frac{1}{2}$ miles in 14 minutes, including an optional stop at Gipping in the case of mixed trains. Mendlesham station had a short siding on the down side and also on the down side was the platform, with a corrugated iron and timber building.

The line now ran due east under the only overbridge constructed: a brick and girder structure carrying the A140 Ipswich-Norwich road. Soon after, the line reached Brockford and Wetheringsett (6 miles)

Cover of the programme for the ceremony of cutting the first sod at "Westerfield Junction", 3 May 1902.

Ticket purchased and annotated by Mr. F. M. Remnant, one of the original Directors.

THE EAST ANGLIAN

The contractors locomotive, "Lady Stevenson", believed taken at Aspall Road, Debenham. in 1903.

HUDSWELL CLARKE

Locomotive No. 1 in makers livery and named.

LOCOMOTIVE PUBLISHING CO.

At Stradbroke about 1909; locomotive No. 3. Note open wagon converted to box wagon.

REAL PHOTOGRAPHS

Mixed train with locomotive No. 1, fitted with longer chimney.

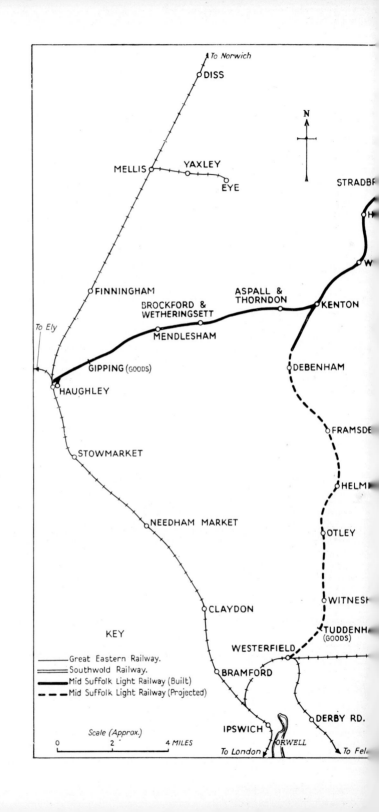

To Norwich

DISS

N

STRADBR

H

W

YAXLEY

MELLIS

EYE

FINNINGHAM

ASPALL &
THORNDON

KENTON

BROCKFORD &
WETHERINGSETT

To Ely

MENDLESHAM

DEBENHAM

GIPPING (GOODS)

HAUGHLEY

FRAMSDE

STOWMARKET

HELMI

NEEDHAM MARKET

OTLEY

WITNESH

CLAYDON

TUDDENH
(GOODS)

KEY

WESTERFIELD

——— Great Eastern Railway.
═══ Southwold Railway.
━━━ Mid Suffolk Light Railway (Built)
━ ━ Mid Suffolk Light Railway (Projected)

BRAMFORD

DERBY RD.

Scale (Approx.)

0   2   4 MILES

IPSWICH

ORWELL

To London

To Fel

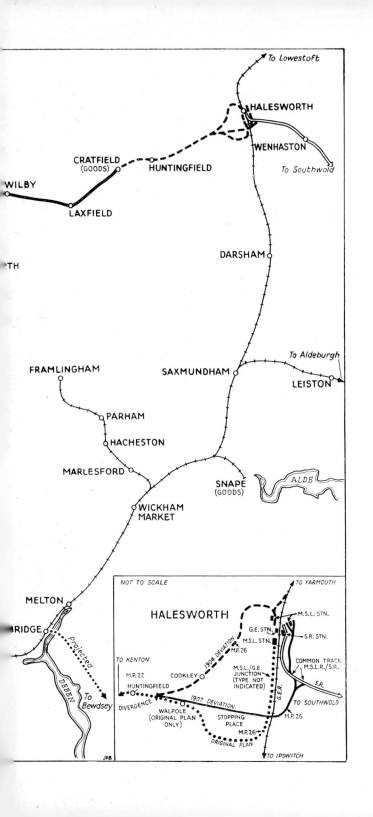

LOCOMOTIVE PUBLISHING CO.

The passenger engine, No. 2, with cattle wagons at Laxfield about 1907.

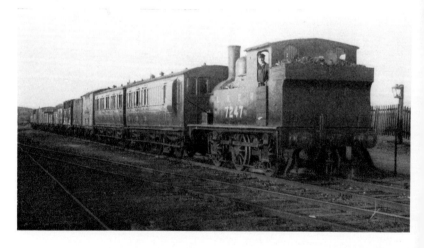

DR. I. C. ALLEN

Mixed train at Haughley with L.N.E.R. 0-6-0T No. 7247 (J65 class), 1932.

Mixed train from Haughley leaving Kenton with 0-6-0T No. 8212.

Afternoon train from Stowmarket going on to branch at Haughley;
B.R. 0-6-0 No. 65467 (J15 class).

At Stradbroke in 1948; J15 0-6-0 No. 5471.

The last working to Laxfield Mill, June 1953; locomotive No. 65388.

generally one of the least-used stations on the line, being more a rail-head than a passenger station, but with a siding and a spur and two small huts on a platform on the up side.

Two and a half miles to the east lay Aspall and Thorndon station, on the road from Debenham to Eye. It was advertised as being "for Debenham" as indeed it was, being some 1½ miles away and further from Thorndon; Aspall was, however, quite near. A "conveyance" met trains at all stations before the grouping, but it was needed most at Aspall whence it carried passengers to surrounding farms. Anyone wishing to travel from Debenham to Ipswich by train would take longer just to get to Haughley than to get all the way to Ipswich by bus. This station, 8½ miles from Haughley, was surprisingly busy as it was the line's central coal depot, but passenger receipts were negligible; some maps of the area did not even show it. The platform and buildings were on the down side.

A further 1½ miles in an easterly direction was Kenton Junction, as the Company hopefully called it. (The only station which really was a junction, Haughley, was rarely referred to as such by the Company). This was one of the busiest stations on the line, only half a mile from the hamlet of Kenton. Although the branch, in terms of track, never extended more than two miles beyond, the station had been equipped with a loop, two platforms, two signals wired to the points (making Kenton the only intermediate station with signals), a shunting spur and five short sidings. A shed with room for one engine only was in use in the early years, in anticipation of the branch services, and *Lady Stevenson* was probably shedded there for some time. This station was also the token exchange point between two sections (a third would have been the Westerfield branch, and the Laxfield-Halesworth line might also have become a section).

Another two miles to the north-east was Worlingworth station, conveniently situated between Worlingworth and Southolt. It had the usual loop and spur and a hut on the platform; in spite of its position the station did not attract much traffic.

The line now turned up a 1 in 44 gradient (the ruling gradient of the line was 1 in 50) northwards to Horham. Traffic here was thin and there was nothing remarkable about the station, which was some ¾ mile south-east of the village on the road from Athelington.

From Horham (14 miles from Haughley) the line bore north, turning east, for another mile over a second underbridge and through a cutting to Stradbroke. In latter days the clerical centre of the line, Stradbroke boasted a staff of two and handled a good deal of traffic in its spur and two sidings; there was a wagon body and a shed on the single platform. The station does not appear to have suffered from being some way from the village.

Wilby station, 1½ miles east of Stradbroke, was one of the smallest stations on the line. Originally it had not been accounted for, but it was opened to all traffic in time for the commencement of passenger services. Like Aspall station, it was literally miles from anywhere and was not originally shown on maps; it dealt with very little traffic; on the platform were a wagon body and another hut.

From here it was another $2\frac{1}{2}$ miles eastwards to Laxfield station in M.S.L.R. days, a hive of activity. There was a small office which had been the Superintendent's, but which became the enginemen's mess when finance was moved to Stradbroke. There was a single platform, a largish shed on the up side and two sidings in an adequate goods yard. Laxfield was, before the grouping, the mechanical headquarters of the system and to the end, minor repairs were done there, although when engines could easily be imported from outside, there was less need to do repairs on the spot. After grouping, the engines were sent to ex-G.E.R. works for overhauls, and Laxfield shed became a sub-shed of Ipswich (32B). Most of the buildings still remain; there were others, among them a smith's shop and an oil store. The station, just outside the village, had a cattle-pen-cum-coal-staithe on the opposite side to the platforms; there were two raised platforms on the up side. The larger, nearer the road, carried most of the buildings while the smaller, towards the engine shed, was not used for passenger traffic but carried a freight shed.

A single line continued across the B1117 and past the water-tower for Laxfield Mills ($19\frac{1}{2}$), where goods traffic was handled from 1906 to 1952. The line continued north-eastward on a line just south of today's electric pylons to a terminus at Cratfield, south-east of the village. This depot, closed in February 1912 after six years of handling freight traffic, was to have been one of the stations for passengers when the system was completed. Virtually nothing was done past this point; probably the uncertainty regarding the possible courses of the line past Huntingfield affected the amount of work carried out.

From Cratfield the line should have continued to Huntingfield ($22\frac{1}{4}$), where a loop was planned. From here three differing routes were planned, as detailed previously.

From Kenton the Debenham branch veered south-west for nearly two miles, crossing a bridge over the B1077 Aspall Road after $1\frac{3}{4}$ miles. The earthworks of the branch continued to the banks of the Deben, some 2 miles from Kenton, just short of the station site. According to the official plans, the line would have continued to stations at Framsden (5), Helmingham (7), Otley ($8\frac{3}{4}$), Witnesham (11), Tuddenham Sidings (12) (mentioned in the Minutes but not marked on the plans) and Westerfield ($13\frac{1}{2}$), where the M.S.L.R. station would be adjacent to that of the G.E.R. with a facing connection.

LOCOMOTIVES AND ROLLING STOCK

The first locomotive to run on M.S.L.R. metals was the contractors' Manning Wardle saddle tank loco, *Lady Stevenson*, as detailed previously. The Board had planned to have only one locomotive and a steam railcar, but they did not pursue the idea far. Three Hudswell Clarke 0-6-0 side-tank engines were ordered by the Company in 1903; two were for delivery as soon as possible and one for when the branch was opened. Nos. 1 and 3 had 3 ft. 4 in. wheels, 12 ft. wheelbase, 14 by 20 in. cylinders, 620 gallon side-tanks and a weight of 29 tons 12 cwt. No. 2 was not quite the same, differing in that it had 13 by 20 in. cylinders, 11 ft. 6 in. wheelbase*, 600 gallon tanks and weighed 24 tons. They were dark red with copper capped chimneys and polished brass domes, and were lettered M.S.L.R.; they bore maker's numbers 711 (built 1904), 723 (built 1905) and 867 (1909). No. 2 had sand-boxes above the frame, the other two below. They apparently had names (and possibly a different livery) when first delivered; it is known that No. 1 was delivered as *Haughley*, and the others were said to be *Kenton* (probably No. 2) and *Laxfield* (probably No. 3). It is not certain that they ever ran carrying names, as photographs taken as early as 1908 show no names. They do not appear to have been very reliable, as on occasion more than one was out of order and the Great Eastern had to lend an engine. From September 1920 to February 1921, a "Blackwall tank", G.E.R. No. 247 (later L.N.E.R. 8213, built in 1893) was lent. The results were so encouraging that after the groupings the M.S.L.R. locos left the branch.

Although the original engines were allocated new L.N.E.R. numbers (1316/7/5) they did not last long: 1315 was scrapped in 1924 without receiving its new number, 1316 withdrawn in November 1928, receiving its new number while retaining its original livery, but 1317 got the full livery at Stratford in 1925, ending its life at Colchester in December 1929.

The natural choice to replace these locos on the branch was the J65 and the first to go were 7153 and 7157. This class sometimes ran on branches as 2-4-0 tanks with the front connecting rods detached, but there is no evidence that they ever ran thus to Laxfield; 7157 survived the Second World War and renumbering to 8212 and was scrapped, fresh from the branch, in November 1947, while 7156, 7253 and 7257 were among others which made up the three locos at Laxfield between the wars.

As these tanks were withdrawn, the first tender engines took over. The J15 class, the oldest ever to work the branch, was ideal for mixed

---

* This may be accounted for by the fact that when first built, it was a 2-4-0T, but whether it ran in this form in service is not certain.

branch work; in the 1940's and '50's they held sway on branch lines throughout East Anglia and soon after the war they came to Laxfield. They managed well, in spite of their length, and at the time of closure, 65388 and 65447 were working the line, having taken over from 65459. 65447 was fitted for working passenger and mixed trains, while 65388 only ran the thrice-weekly freight trains; 65467 also hauled occasional trains.

The original passenger carriages were, as already stated, six ex-Metropolitan District Railway two-class four-wheelers; some had centre gangways, and three were fitted with acetylene gas plants. There was also one passenger brake and three parcels vans, all of which were four-wheelers. At some time after the grouping these were replaced by G.E.R. six-wheel compartment stock and this in turn was superseded by G.E.R. suburban six-wheelers with "cattle-truck" partitioned in the third-class compartments. There was normally a two-car rake including both classes, although third-class only trains ran occasionally in independent days when up to six coaches were used if needed. After grouping, two coaches was generally the maximum; but towards the end of the line's career, two 2-coach sets were on the line, and for the last week they were coupled together.

The Company possessed 21 miscellaneous freight vehicles at the grouping, running them on its own lines and into the exchange sidings. When the L.N.E.R. introduced through running, wagons came at random, but they still had to be shunted at Haughley exchange sidings. There were some kept on the branch for local use, and in L.N.E.R. days there was a through milk van daily to Bishopsgate.

TRAIN SERVICES

The earliest passenger timetable extant is that of Summer 1911, when the following passenger and mixed trains ran:

MO	6.40 a.m.	ex Laxfield	arr. Haughley	7.47
MX	8.20 a.m.	ex Laxfield	arr. Haughley	9.27
TuFO	12.10 p.m.	ex Kenton	arr. Haughley	12.52
MSO	12.00 p.m.	ex Laxfield	arr. Haughley	1.14
	3.20 p.m.	ex Laxfield	arr. Haughley	4.37

SUNDAYS

7.00 a.m.	ex Laxfield	arr. Haughley	8.07
5.17 p.m.	ex Laxfield	arr. Haughley	6.27

	10.00 a.m.	ex Haughley	arr. Laxfield	11.02
SX	2.37 p.m.	ex Haughley	arr. Kenton	3.25
SO	3.00 p.m.	ex Haughley	arr. Laxfield	4.29
	5.55 p.m.	ex Haughley	arr. Laxfield	7.00

SUNDAYS

8.50 a.m.	ex Haughley	arr. Laxfield	9.52
7.35 p.m.	ex Haughley	arr. Laxfield	8.37

Conveyances (most of them traps) met passengers at each station by each train and conveyed them to all neighbouring villages. Each village had its own trap and details were printed on the Company timetable handbills. By 1920 the Sunday morning train had been abolished and all the three trains (8.15, 1.00, 3.25 ex-Laxfield and the 10.5, 12.55 and 5.30 ex-Haughley) ran all the way on weekdays. Conveyances (most of them now motor) could be summoned, but now by request only. The short workings from Kenton to Haughley had been withdrawn before the war and the Kenton loco shed fell into disuse soon after, the only booked short workings after this being those to Aspall mentioned below. That winter the 1.00 ex-Laxfield and 5.30 ex-Haughley were both retimed, and the former and the 12.55 ex-Haughley ran on Tuesdays and Thursdays only, carrying only third class passengers.

The Sunday train finally disappeared in 1921, but the weekday service was improved. Trains left Laxfield at 7.35 (8.10 on Tuesdays), 11.5 (third class only) and 3.25, and Haughley at 9.40, 12.55 (third) and 5.40. Journeys now took some ten minutes longer than in 1911 as extra traffic caused more shunting. In summer 1922 the third class trains were opened to both classes, and the 12.55 and 5.40 ex-Haughley retimed. An extra train left Haughley at 8.55 p.m. on Saturdays.

After the groupings, timetables became more complicated, with separate schedules for Tuesdays (when most freight was carried), and in 1924 the following trains ran, two locomotives being in use on these duties with another in reserve:

Duty A (*Weekdays*)

	11.05 a.m.	ex Laxfield	mixed	arr. Haughley	12.10
	1.00 p.m.	ex Haughley	mixed	arr. Laxfield	2.05
	3.25 p.m.	ex Laxfield	passenger	arr. Haughley	4.40
SX	5.40 p.m.	ex Haughley	passenger	arr. Laxfield	6.45
SO	6.05 p.m.	ex Haughley	passenger	arr. Laxfield	7.10

Duty B (*TuX*)

7.35 a.m.	ex Laxfield	mixed	arr. Haughley	8.40
9.40 a.m.	ex Haughley	mixed	arr. Laxfield	10.45
12.00 n'n	ex Laxfield	freight to Aspall		
2.55 p.m.	ex Aspall	freight to Laxfield		

When freight traffic was heavy, the 12 noon ex-Laxfield ran through to Haughley, returning to Laxfield at 2.55 p.m.

Duty C (*TuO*)

3.55 a.m.	ex Laxfield	cattle and goods to Haughley		
6.15 a.m.	ex Haughley	freight to Laxfield		
8.10 a.m.	ex Laxfield	mixed	arr. Haughley	9.15
9.40 a.m.	ex Haughley	mixed	arr. Laxfield	10.45

This timetable was not basically different from the previous one; the passenger and mixed trains are much the same but accelerated. The Tuesdays only 9.40 ex-Haughley was retimed first to 9.48 and then to 9.45, and the 8.10 (TuO) ex-Laxfield to 8.5. The market traffic declined in the 30's and by the outbreak of war the separate Tuesday table had been abolished; although the fall in goods traffic caused less shunting, Mixed trains were slower and passenger trains slower still.

The emergency timetables of October 1939 set the pattern of operation for the last thirteen years by finally reducing the number of passenger-carrying trains to two, which left Laxfield at 7.25 and 2.30 and Haughley at 11.0 and 4.50. Only one engine was in use for much of the time and times were increased, the 11.0 from Haughley taking two hours for 19 miles.

Things had improved a little by the winter 1946/7 timetable, when the following trains were scheduled:

7.45 a.m.	ex Laxfield	arr. Haughley	9.00
11.08 a.m.	ex Haughley	arr. Laxfield	12.40
1.50 p.m.	ex Laxfield	arr. Haughley	3.20
3.54 p.m.	ex Haughley	arr. Laxfield	5.09

Extra trains were sometimes run on summer evenings before the war to connect with trains for Liverpool Street. Through trains for schoolchildren occasionally ran through to Stowmarket. At the time of closure, the following trains ran on weekdays only:

| ex Haughley | 11.15, 3SO55, 4SX42 |
| ex Laxfield | 7.21, 1.45 |

Although passenger traffic in the last week was heavy and crowds appeared to see the last train, freight traffic was negligible and mixed trains carried hardly any freight.

One of the original disadvantages of freight working over the line was the load restriction caused by the heavy gradient. In latter days it was rarely reached, but special precautions had to be taken when traffic had been heavy. On down goods trains, the loco could take only 14 waggons from Haughley to Gipping and 21 the rest of the way (there was no restriction on Athelington bank), while on up trains one engine could take 21 wagons all the way. As a rule, trains were mixed, although there were always a few scheduled freight trains (see above). By 1951 only the morning trains were mixed, but there was a special freight working on Mondays, Wednesdays and Fridays hauled by 65388, leaving Laxfield at 10.15 a.m., reaching Haughley at 12.45 and returning at 1.30.

From the opening of the line in 1904, a daily freight train ran, leaving Haughley at 8.00, arriving at Laxfield 11.15, returning 1.00 to reach Haughley at 4.15. In addition, unofficial goods workings ran on the Debenham line and they were probably worked by *Lady Stevenson* as the track was of poor standard.

In the 1920's nine or ten goods vehicles plus a guard's van would generally be attached to mixed trains, and there were probably more in the last war, when bombs and other military equipment were carried to Mendlesham airfield. At the end, this had fallen to four or five, although more wagons were carried on freight-only trains. At the peak of the line's popularity, 600 head of cattle weekly were carried, and there was much through traffic to Ipswich and Bishopsgate, including the milk van. All this had to go through the exchange sidings. Probably the heaviest traffic carried in later years was that on the final lifting train.

As there was no turntable on the branch, which had been built with tank operation in mind, all tender engines had to operate a push-and-pull service. Such a service on a long, steep branch with mixed trains and shunting at intermediate stations would seem to present considerable difficulties. The crews of shed 32B managed, however, to run an accelerated service of mixed trains after the war in spite of more complicated shunting manoeuvres.

MISCELLANEOUS

The Mid-Suffolk Light Railway was originally laid with 30 ft. Vignoles rail weighing 56 lb. per yard, with staggered joints. Although the line remained classified as a light railway until its closure (in the Eastern Region timetable it was specifically mentioned), the lightweight rail was replaced as necessary by standard L.N.E.R. rail. The signals and the points on running lines were worked on ground frames and the signals wired to the points. The signals were the Haughley down starter (M.S.L.R., when trains started from the bay they were governed by main line signals), the Kenton up and down starters (junction signals do not appear to have been erected), and the Laxfield up starter, which was apparently removed early.

Four hundred yards from Laxfield station on the Mills line was the water system. It had not been included in the plans and the contractors had not erected a tower; as the area was apparently not surveyed for suitable arrangements, a makeshift contraption was put up; it remained till the end. A petrol pumping engine of great antiquity and irregular habits pumped water from a pond into an overhead tank, but in the summer the pond dried up and a nearby stream had to be damned. Trains must have run to the water tower before the Cratfield extension was officially opened; otherwise water would have had to come in buckets.

At Kenton there was another automatic pumping engine, while at Haughley (M.S.L.R.) there was a petrol engine operating through a walking beam, by the coal staithe. After the grouping the G.E.R. supply was used.

All ten passenger stations had public rooms of some sort while eight had lock-up sheds or rooms, and another eight had loading bays; every station except the old Haughley (East) station had a cattle pen. This was because cattle, although the staple traffic of the line, were carried mainly for markets beyond Haughley, where there was not much apart from a station, and the cattle did not need to leave the trucks there while in transit.

Station nameboards and permanent speed restriction signs on the line had a unique style of lettering, and those from Kenton are preserved in the yard of the British Transport Museum at Clapham. Station buildings were painted in the company's grey livery; even now, ten years after closure, station buildings at Laxfield are still intact, and the course of the line can be plainly seen. Even the earthworks of sections lifted in the Great War are still there, and the Debenham bridge is almost intact.

The first fare list of 1911 shows a minimum fare from Haughley only fares from Haughley are quoted) of 4½d. third class single to Mendlesham; in other words, third class fares were 1d. per mile and first class fares just over 2d. per mile. The highest fare quoted was a period return first class from Haughley to Laxfield, which cost 5s. 3d., third class cheap day returns were available on Market Day (Tuesday) to Haughley by the first up train only for one and a half times the single fare. On Saturdays returns at one and a quarter times the single fare were issued to Haughley for return on the Saturday, Sunday or Monday. Cheap returns could be obtained on Sundays at a minimum of 6d. to any station, returning on the Sunday or Monday. For children under twelve or three or over, fares were halved, with fractions of 1d. counting as 1d. on cheap day returns.

By 1920 most concessions had been abolished as the passenger service began to contract. The market fare was available by the second up train only to Haughley, these concessions applying to third class passengers only. In 1922 this was altered by the introduction of cheap day four-thirds single fare returns on Tuesdays to Ipswich and on Thursdays to Stowmarket. These were soon followed by weekend returns between Mid-Suffolk and G.E.R. stations at the same rate at a minimum of 5/- for third class tickets. Fractions of 3d. were charged as 3d. On Saturdays, cheap day and half-day tickets were available to Haughley; in summer, excursion tickets were available as required to main stations in East Anglia. Normally, through bookings were available to Stowmarket, Ipswich and Liverpool Street. After grouping, normal L.N.E.R. and B.R. fare scales applied. M.S.L.R. tickets were of pink card.

As the line was single track throughout, except at stations, and a light railway, neither visual semaphore signals nor fences were necessary as long as only one engine was in steam in each section, but a staff was required. The line was divided into two sections after 1912: Haughley-Kenton and Kenton-Laxfield, the staffs being kept at Kenton. The signals at Kenton, although not junction type, were intended for use when the branch was opened. Each of the sections was governed by the novel single divided staff. Each staff had two halves, padlocked together except when two trains went through the section in the same direction, as happened thrice weekly in latter days.

The line was generally free from accidents, except at the numerous level crossings, as after the line was taken over by the L.N.E.R. crossing keepers were "retired" as part of an economy drive, and residents and station staff helped the train crews with the crossings. From time to time one of the numerous occupation crossings would be occupied or left open when a train came and in time this line achieved a reputation somewhat similar to that now enjoyed by the Totton, Hythe and Fawley. The number of ungated level crossings increased steadily as a result of accidents.

The staff of the railway in independent days was comparatively top-heavy. The original directors of the Company were: F. S. Stevenson, M.P. (Chairman), The Earl of Stradbroke (Vice-Chairman),

J. B. Chevallier, J.P., D. F. Goddard, M.P., and B. M. Kilby. Mr. Kilby resigned almost straight away and after November 1901, J. T. Cobbold and F. M. Remnant joined the board. Mr. Goddard resigned soon after, and in March 1906, Mr. Stevenson resigned, as already stated, to be replaced as Chairman by the Earl of Stradbroke. At the time of absorption, only Messrs. Remnant and Chevallier were still holding office.

The first group of senior employees consisted of H. L. Godden (Traffic Manager), H. J. Rednal (Assistant Manager), H. R. Gillingwater (Superintendent after 1904), T. H. Bryant (Local Secretary), and C. D. Szlumper (Engineer from 1905). The first Secretary was N. P. Jaffrey, who resigned in February 1902; E. H. Messeder took over and handed in his resignation in February 1904; as there was some question of moving the offices of the company, it was refused, but W. Warren was appointed Acting Secretary. He took over in November and acted as Receiver from October 1906 to February 1907. Then he resigned the Receivership, but he remained Secretary until 1912. In 1922, only Mr. Gillingwater remained in office on the spot. Major J. F. R. Daniel was receiver until 1918, when A. P. Parker, Assistant Manager of the Great Eastern, took over. W. Lindsey-Badcock was General Superintendent and Engineer from 1913 to 1923. T. J. Dalgleish was Assistant Superintendent and Accountant after May 1905 and Acting Superintendent from early 1924.

Around sixty men were employed in the line's heyday. Each station was staffed by one "signal porter", except for Stradbroke, where there was a stationmaster as well as a clerk to deal with finance.

The Mid-Suffolk kept some of its individuality right to the end. Dr. Ian Allen describes how the two goods guards used to keep their own vans, and when the goods from Laxfield crossed the mixed at Kenton, some complicated shunting ensured that when the guards exchanged trains there, they also exchanged vans. The result was that the up goods left on the down line and the down passenger on the up line, without benefit of signals, which were only used when officers from outside were visiting. Dr. Allen also relates that when an officer's special car ran in 1951 (a J15 with the Ipswich six-wheeled saloon), nobody could enjoy the lunch provided, as they could not understand the method of working with split staff, and expected to meet a train going the other way at any moment.

Nowadays public transport in the area is mainly left to the Eastern Counties Bus Company, who have a network of bus routes throughout the county, over some of the most awkward roads in England. Bus services are adequate and to a certain extent cover the loss inflicted by the withdrawal of train services.

To give some idea of where the traffic came from when the line was young, some figures are quoted from the M.S.L.R. receipts book. They apply to all traffic.

	OCTOBER 1908				JUNE 1921			
	£	s.	d.	%	£	s.	d.	%
Aspall	18	17	8	9	7	19	6	6
Haughley	57	15	0	25	52	19	6	43
Kenton	18	7	2	8	6	19	8½	6
Laxfield	79	7	8	34	29	2	5¼	24
Mendlesham	22	16	0	10	5	11	0¼	5
Stradbroke	34	10	7	14	20	15	5½	16
TOTAL ...	£231	14	1		£123	7	8	

Even if one makes allowances for the fact that the first are for the first full month of passenger operation, the comparisons between the two is alarming. The receipts of the smaller stations (Gipping, Brockford, Horham and Wilby) are included in the figures for the nearest station to them.

DISTANCE TABLE OF THE MID-SUFFOLK RAILWAY

Miles

	HAUGHLEY (East), HAUGHLEY (West) stations and Exchange sidings
$\frac{1}{4}$	Underbridge one
$2\frac{1}{4}$	Gipping (Old Newton) siding
$4\frac{1}{2}$	Mendlesham station
$5\frac{1}{2}$	A140 Overbridge
6	Brockford and Wetheringsett station
$8\frac{1}{2}$	Aspall and Thorndon station
10	Kenton Junction and station
12	Worlingworth station
14	Horham station
$14\frac{1}{4}$	Underbridge two
15	Stradbroke station
$16\frac{1}{2}$	Wilby station
19	LAXFIELD STATION
$19\frac{1}{4}$	Laxfield Water Tower
$19\frac{1}{2}$	Laxfield Mills Siding
21	CRATFIELD Siding
-	KENTON JUNCTION
$1\frac{3}{4}$	B1077 Underbridge
$2\frac{1}{4}$	End of works

Lines on which construction was ordered to begin

Miles

-	WESTERFIELD STATION(S) and Junction
$1\frac{1}{2}$	Tuddenham siding
$2\frac{1}{2}$	Witnesham
$4\frac{3}{4}$	Otley
$6\frac{1}{2}$	Helmingham
$8\frac{1}{2}$	Framsden
11	Debenham
$11\frac{1}{4}$	Beginning of works
$13\frac{1}{2}$	KENTON JUNCTION

Cratfield-Halesworth (Original Plan)

Miles

-	CRATFIELD STATION
$1\frac{1}{4}$	Huntingfield station
$3\frac{1}{4}$	Walpole station
6	Halesworth South Junction
$6\frac{1}{2}$	HALESWORTH STATION (M.S.L.R.)

(1904 *Deviation*)

Miles
- CRATFIELD STATION
1¼ Huntingfield station
4 Cookley (or Walpole) station
5¾ HALESWORTH STATION (M.S.L.R.) and junction

(1907 *Deviation*)

Miles
- CRATFIELD STATION
1¾ Huntingfield station
4¾ "Stopping place"
5 Flyover crossing G.E.R. at right angles
5½ Southwold Spur junction
   Junctions with Southwold line
6 HALESWORTH STATION (M.S.L.R.)

Total Length Constructed

Haughley-Kenton	...	10 miles
Westerfield Branch	...	2¼ ,,
Kenton-Halesworth	...	11 ,,
TOTAL	... ...	23¼ ,,

Total Length Proposed but not Constructed from Westerfield to Huntingfield

Westerfield Branch	...	11¼ miles
Cratfield-Huntingfield	...	1¼ ,,
TOTAL	... ...	12½ ,,

Length of track east of Huntingfield

Original plan	... ...	5¾ miles
1904 plan	... ...	4¾ ,,
1907 plan	... ...	5 ,,

Total Length west of Huntingfield*

Constructed	... ...	23¼ miles
Proposed ...	... ...	12½ ,,
TOTAL	... ...	35¾ ,,

Total Length Planned

Original route	... ...	41½ miles
With 1904 deviation	...	40½ ,,
With 1907 deviation	...	40¾ ,,

* This point is only taken for convenience. The alternative routes actually divided about one mile east of Huntingfield.

28

BIBLIOGRAPHY

EASTERN REGION MAGAZINE, November 1952, p. 213. A concise account of the closure, with a picture.

0-6-0 TANKS OF THE G.E.R., P. Proud, R.C.T.S., 1954. Mainly about *Blackwall tanks*, with several photos, but none of the Mid-Suffolk. M.S.L.R. mentioned in connection with locos operated around the grouping.

RAILWAY MAGAZINE, July-December 1924, p. 347 et seq., by J. F. Gairns. Details of the first twenty years with many photos.

March 1937: Questions answered concerning finance.

September 1952, p. 638: Short article referring to closure.

October 1957, December 1962: Questions answered.

RAILWAYS (now *Railway World*), July 1952, pp. 161/8. Two short articles by W. A. Camwell, the first in the "Around the branch lines" series dealing with the termini, the second in the series "Some shed scenes to remember". Three photographs and concise text.

STANDARD GAUGE LIGHT RAILWAYS and THE LIGHT RAILWAY HANDBOOK, by R. W. Kidner (Oakwood Press), p. 39. Concise note-form history with one photo.

THE BRANCH LINE ALBUM, Whitehouse, Ian Allan, 1962. One photo with short caption.

TRAINS ILLUSTRATED (now *Modern Railways*), October 1952, pp. 374/6/7/3 (in that order), by R. E. Vincent. History, with details of last days of operation. Several photos.

WILDINGS OF SHREWSBURY LTD.